Magnetic Mondays

The Real Secret to Attracting the Career you Want

Magnetic Mondays
Copyright © 2018 by Mariana Pachai

ISBN 978-1-999-40160-3
Printed in Canada

Table of Contents

Preface

For many years in my career, I was unhappy, bitter and depressed. I didn't like what I was doing, and I didn't like the people that I was working with. I felt like my dreams were fading. I had no idea how to grow professionally, regain balance and manage stress.

I knew I need to decide if I was going to sink or swim. So, I changed my outlook, became positive, and took action. I challenged myself to extend beyond what I knew by doing research, networking, and asking a lot of questions. Fast forward to today, I am an accomplished author, HR consultant, and founder of Pave Your Path Career Transformation Coaching. Most importantly, I am very satisfied with the person that I am becoming.

I believe that you too can find satisfaction in the work you do and in the lives you impact. This book is for you if you feel stuck, demotivated, or bored in your career. Learn how to attract the things you want, start the week with a positive attitude and look forward to crafting your trade, gaining new experiences, and building new relationships. I want you to create your own opportunities and focus on bringing about positive and radical change in your own life. By doing this, you will start to attract the right people and opportunities.

But you can't be positive about something you don't like, so together with this book, we will devise a plan towards doing what you like. You'll have a whole new meaning to Mondays!

It starts with believing in yourself, changing your mindset, and taking action.

Magnetic Mondays
The Real Secret to Attracting the Career you Want

Introduction

Why do we work? Apart from the paycheck, what is the compelling reason for dragging ourselves out of bed each morning? Most of us work to have the financial means to support ourselves and our families because without financial freedom, we cannot design the life we want. Work forms a significant part of our identity and those without jobs tend to lose self-respect or even go into a phase of depression. If you have ever lost a job or struggled to find a job you would understand these sentiments. Work provides opportunities for us to identify our strengths, explore our potential and develop them as we interact with people to pursue shared goals. Through our work, we feel that we contribute to society and to the world at large. Work gives us the important means to develop and maintain immeasurable assets for life. These include relationships, diverse networks, and individual transformation.

According to psychologist professor, Barry Schwartz, we feel accomplished when we are in charge of our own work and not subject to the decisions forced on us. When we feel we can control what and how we work, we become productive and find work fun and meaningful. Satisfied workers are engaged by their work and they lose themselves in it. Not all the time of course, but often enough for that to be obvious to them. It forces them to stretch themselves and to go outside their comfort zones. For satisfied workers, the subject of money almost never comes up.

The average person will spend approximately 90,000 hours at work over their lifetime. For many of us, this will be most of our lives. Of course, the amount of time spent working will vary from person to person depending on many different factors. However, it is safe to say that our job can have a huge impact on our quality of life. For this reason, it is pivotal that we spend this time doing something we truly enjoy—work that is spent living out our purpose.

I am a huge advocate of introspection and I honestly believe that most of the answers we seek are right there within us. That's why I want you to shift your focus on to bringing about positive and radical change in your own life, so that you can start attracting the right people and opportunities.

Mondays set the precedent for the rest of your week. They mark the beginning of something fresh and brand new. You get to decide how you want to start the week, with a positive attitude or with one of resistance and disdain. Unless you change your perception about Mondays, your thoughts, actions and outcomes will always be the same. Try to think positively and don't let unhappiness or sadness be associated with Mondays. Instead, look at Mondays as the starting point of productivity. Then use this productivity and momentum to tackle all of those unfinished projects that have been holding you down.

In this book, I identify numerous ways of attracting your ideal career by first looking within and working on you, as I truly believe all our success stems from our ability to first know and understand ourselves.

Chapter
1
Mindset

Your mindset is simply your way of thinking, which in turn determines your behavior. Your attitude is how you feel about something. Your mindset shapes your attitude, and your attitude reinforces your mindset. In other words, the thinking patterns you routinely adopt largely govern the results you achieve. Therefore, if you really want to start attracting the right situations in your life you need to start with your thinking.

If you are reading this book, chances are things don't fall into place in your life and, if they do, they're not the way you intend them to be. But making a conscious effort to change your thoughts can be a big step in the right direction. If you cannot believe it and visualize it, it is impossible to make it happen. Could you imagine trying to sell a product you did not believe in? Would you be able to convince others that it was good for them if you did not believe it yourself? Likewise, you need to start believing in your own dreams and abilities. You need to eliminate areas of doubt and self-manipulation.

The mind is a powerful thing; most of our battles are first won or lost in the mind. That is the power you hold, the power of choice and the power to own every decision you make whether good or bad. The power is not lost due to bad breaks, bad relationships or missed opportunities. You are responsible for your choices and the way your life turns out—so start being aware of the decisions you are making. Forget the past and be in the present, this is your moment to excel!

Agnes Kowalski, wealth therapist and mindset coach says that, "Mindset is 95% of how you create your external reality. Whatever you are thinking about in your career is what you are manifesting in your current reality." Start with paying attention to your thoughts throughout the day and look at your areas of focus. Try to pay attention to your areas of struggle or weakness. Are you constantly worried, anxious or perplexed? Write these thoughts down for one week and then, on another sheet of paper, write down the things you would like to focus on and think about instead. Try to be as precise as possible when making these notes. For example, Monday – 8 a.m.: "Feeling anxious about work today, I have a packed day and I am not sure how I will get it all done. Monday 11:45 a.m., worried about the mortgage payment that is coming due—this is my priority and that means no dining out again this month."

Now on a separate list, write down, "I am so fortunate to have a partner who supports my dreams. I think I will spend the next few weeks working on a vision board for how I want our life to be. I think I want us to be able to save for our kid's college. I want us to save enough to retire by the beach. I better start researching and looking for some ways I could start working towards this. Perhaps we could start renting out the basement or maybe I can sign up to coach tennis a few hours a week. I love playing tennis and I know this would be a great way to keep fit."

By doing this you will begin to shift your thoughts and habits. Changing a habit is nothing more than simultaneously weakening one neural pathway and strengthening another (perhaps new) pathway. Neural pathways operate like muscles; they get stronger with use and weaker when neglected. Instead of being consumed with worry and anxiety you will begin to spark new ideas and passion for a better and happier life.

Another way to change your mindset about Mondays is to plan an activity around this day. We tend to perceive weekends as fun and exciting because we plan most of our fun activities around these two days. But what if you took a couple hours out of your work week to do something you could look forward to? Perhaps plan to meet up for dinner with an old friend, plan a paint night with a couple of friends, plan to go to a networking event or plan to meet with a client or business partner on a Monday. This will give you a good reason to leave the office on time and evoke feelings of anticipation because it is something you want to do and will enjoy doing.

"People with higher levels of well-being are 31% more productive at work and 87% less likely to quit" - World Economic Forum. Try exercising for 20 minutes and meditating for 10 minutes every day; exercising will get your heart rate up and release those happy hormones while meditating will silence your thoughts and bring about peace and tranquility in your life regardless of what is going on around you. I know we are all pressed for time, especially when we have other commitments such as family or studies, but try to make time for self-care. How and where you choose to do it is up to you. Should you decide to do it on your own there are lots of self-guided articles and videos out there on meditation and exercising. If you need the extra motivation join a gym that carries both services.

If you haven't already, adopt a growth mindset. To briefly sum up: individuals who believe their talents can be developed (through hard work, good strategies, and input from others) have a growth mindset. They tend to achieve more than those with a more fixed mindset (those who believe their talents are innate gifts). This is because they worry less about looking smart and they put more energy into learning. Most importantly, individuals with growth mindsets seize the moment and roll with the punches.

Fake it till you make it!

I am sure you've heard of the term "Fake it till you make it". It is used to suggest that, by imitating confidence, competence, and an optimistic mindset, a person can realize those qualities in their real life. Researchers have found that "acting" a certain way allows your brain to "rehearse" a new way of thinking and can set off a desired chain of events in the future. Here are two scientifically-backed strategies for "faking" your way to a better job.

1. **Act before you think:** Tim Wilson from the University of Virginia found that the best way to change our identity is to change our behavior first. If you want to get over your fear of public speaking, then you actually need to speak. If you want to make more friends at work, you will probably have to engage in small talk. The weather always seems to be something people like to talk about—whether it's a nice sunny day out or cold blustery day. You can initiate the conversation with "Isn't it a nice day out today?" or "What crazy weather today, eh?"

   Vincent Van Gogh pretty much summed it up by saying, "If you hear a voice within you say 'you cannot paint', then by all means paint, and that voice will be silenced."

2. **Pretend to know the answer:** In many cases, thinking that we are limited is itself a limiting factor. When you are presented with a difficult question, don't let your first thought be, *I don't know the answer to this,* instead allow yourself some time to think and learn. There is accumulating evidence which suggests that our thoughts are often capable of extending our cognitive and physical limits. Herminia Ibarra writes in the *Harvard Business Review*, "By viewing ourselves as works in progress, we multiply our capacity to learn, avoid being pigeonholed, and ultimately become better leaders. We're never too experienced to fake it till we learn it."

Bear in mind this theory does not suggest that you need to pretend to be someone you are not. The most important thing is that what you are faking is aligned to your vision, values and goals.

Always choose to emulate your true authentic self and the person you hope to become. In so doing, take actionable steps to be that person and practise mindfulness, the act of being aware. If you are not being true to you, you are not making it—you are only fakin' it!

End of chapter exercise:

Forget The "To-Do" List, You Need A 'Stop Doing' List

Later in the book we will talk about creating a list of Things to Do. However, I want you to start off with first listing some things that you should STOP doing.

Here is my Stop-Doing List:

1. Stop complaining
2. Stop blaming other people
3. Stop being late
4. Stop being bitter
5. Stop scrolling through social media aimlessly

Now you list 5 things you think you should quit or stop doing:

1. ___________________________
2. ___________________________
3. ___________________________
4. ___________________________
5. ___________________________

If you are comfortable with all of your habits, you can skip this exercise.

Chapter
2
Vision, Values & Purpose

A vision is a proclamation of what you want to accomplish for yourself in the near future and your value is based on your judgement of what is important in life. Our vision, values and purpose are very personal declarations. They can be inspired but should never be swayed by others. Many times, we lose sight of these three important things or we forget to take a moment to consider what really matters to us. But how can we attract the right situations if we don't really know what we want? In this chapter, I want you to take a moment to identify your values and vision for your life. Begin by identifying five of your most important values.

To get you started, below I have listed some of my core values.

1. Freedom

2. Community

3. Making a Difference

4. Integrity

5. Personal Expression

Now you list your five most important values:

1.______________________________

2.______________________________

3.______________________________

4.______________________________

5.______________________________

Vision in your career

Writing a career vision statement is making a commitment to live your life in a certain way, drawing from the many complexities that make you who you are—like your relationships, belief systems and values, health, well-being, and personality.

Of course, your career vision statement can also change over time, depending on how you grow and what is happening in your life. But for now, we will focus on what you are feeling right now. Write statements about the future you envision as if you are already making them happen. The more detailed you make your image the better you can see it in your mind's eye.

Here is an example of a personal vision statement I came across recently: "My career is motivating and diverse with opportunity for challenge and growth. I see the people I work with as individuals I can be open with, learn from and help. Each day brings excitement and opportunity for building relationships, solving problems and creating opportunities." Bear in mind that the vision statement is an idea and hope for what this individual wants and hopes for in her career. It is not her current situation, but it creates a vivid image of what she would like her career to look like. Similarly, you should think about five things you want to manifest in your career and from this build your vision statement.

Now write your vision for your career:

____

____

____

Purpose in life comes from doing what we love through meaningful work. Your purpose is your why! By digging into your thoughts, looking at your values and vision you will begin to unearth your purpose. Your heart is the best tool for guiding you towards your purpose and passion. Therefore, ask yourself, "What do I enjoy doing?" There are no rules here, you don't have to have one purpose in life, there can be as many as you can handle and are passionate about.

Chapter
3
Self-awareness & Mindfulness

The psychological study of self-awareness can be traced back to 1972 when psychologists Shelley Duval and Robert Wicklund developed the theory of self-awareness. They proposed that, "when we focus our attention on ourselves, we evaluate and compare our current behavior to our internal standards and values. We become self-conscious as objective evaluators of ourselves." Essentially, they consider self-awareness as a major mechanism of self-control. Most of us tunnel through life completely disconnected from ourselves. We spend most of our time working to accumulate stuff, without ever taking the time to consider our emotions and experiences.

Stress affects our ability to concentrate and increases the likelihood of developing medical and psychological disorders. Mindfulness helps control our reaction to stress, which in turn results in positive mental health.

The term mindfulness says it all —the act of being aware. It means to fully be present and to take a moment to observe everything that surrounds us in this precise moment, from our thoughts to our emotions, our feelings, our surroundings, and the way our body feels.

Use mindfulness to increase your self-awareness and effectiveness by:

1. Creating some space for yourself—leave some time in the day to spend with yourself, either reflecting on your thoughts, reading a book or journaling.

2. Practising mindfulness. You can practise mindfulness anywhere and at any time you want, through mindful listening, mindful eating or walking.

3. Practising listening. In this case you want to practise being present and paying attention to other people's emotions, body movement and language. It is about showing empathy and understanding without constantly evaluating or judging. Listen to other people in order to first understand then respond.

4. Embracing feedback & criticism - Sometimes we can be too afraid to ask what others think of us – yes sometimes the feedback may be biased or even dishonest, but you will be able to differentiate them from real, genuine and balanced feedback as you learn more about yourself and others.

It is through practising mindfulness that we gain more control of our emotions and reactions to situations. In other words, our emotions should not be impacted by someone else's behavior. This one is especially difficult and takes a lot of practice. Imagine sitting at the stop light and the guy behind you starts honking, indicating that you should start moving. Now, he does not have visibility of the road, but he decides that you are holding him back with those 10–15 seconds that you took to move. Your whole mood for the day could change because of this unfavorable encounter.

Mirroring people who are angry almost seems like a natural reflex. Imagine having a conversation with a co-worker or a boss who is angry for some reason. You, being unsure about the source of their anger, decide that you are now angry too. Perhaps the conversation got heated or you felt blamed for the situation. Regardless of the conversation and who it is with, we have control over how we react to situations. How we react when faced against a storm will determine whether we stay afloat or sink. Be confident and bold enough to speak your mind, but try not to let your emotions take over.

Like most things, mindfulness is a choice and it is also a discipline. It is a skill that we can master slowly over time as it teaches us how to be more self-aware and less reactive to negative events or stimuli.

Chapter
4
Goals

Goals form one of the cornerstones in our career. They provide a visual and mental roadmap of where we want to be in life. Pablo Picasso said it best, "Our goals can only be reached through a vehicle of a plan, in which we must fervently believe, and upon which we must vigorously act. There is no other route to success." Imagine if you had no plan at all. It would be as if you were running around like a headless chicken, with no sense of direction. Then imagine if you had a plan but no will or passion to act.

Look at the goals you have in place in your life—do they make you feel alive? Do they represent the highest version of you? Will you be proud of yourself for attaining them? Do they inspire you? Are your goals achievable or are they so far down the rabbit hole that they hold no zeal for you because you can't even believe in your ability to attain them?

Goals help us to identify the things we want in life and then plan for how we will achieve them. As a result, your goals should be an extension of who you are and what you care about. If your goals are in conflict with your authentic values and beliefs, you won't achieve them. You'll unconsciously sabotage the path to these goals because, deep down, the attainment of them feels wrong. Or you'll break yourself in the effort to bring about the goal only to wake up with the realization that what you're left with is shallow and meaningless.

Be SMART about your goals and get them down in a journal or in a digital notebook. Ensure that they are **S**pecific, **M**easurable, **A**chievable, **R**elevant and **T**ime Bound. There are a lot of guides and worksheets on the internet on writing SMART goals. Be sure to use one to document your next set of goals. But, before you start with new ones, begin with writing down those goals you already have in your head or those ones you have already started working on.

SMART GOALS

Example:

Overarching goal: Get a new job as a financial advisor in a major bank.	
Specific	I will work in as financial advisor with a major bank in the Greater Toronto Area.
Measurable	I will apply to 2 job postings every day and attend at least 2 interviews per month.
Attainable	I can commit my time to applying to 2 jobs in the evening and I can attend interviews as the need arises.
Relevant	I will finally be able earn the income I want and live out my lifelong dream of helping people invest their money to reach their financial goals.
Time-Bound	I will be hired within 3 months.
Final goal: I will become a financial advisor with a major bank in the next 3 months. I will accomplish this by applying to 2 jobs each day and attending at least 2 interviews each month.	

End of chapter exercise:

Maybe your goal isn't to find a new job. Perhaps you want to write a book, volunteer, learn to swim, take a professional development course or start a side hustle. Let's set a goal to get you focused.

Use the template below to write your next goal.

<table>
<tr><td>Overarching goal:

</td></tr>
</table>

SMART Goals Worksheet

Specific	What do you want to accomplish? (who, what, when, where, how)
Measurable	How will you track your progress?
Attainable	Will you be able to achieve this goal? Is it realistic?
Relevant	How does this goal matter to you? Why are you doing this?
Time-Bound	When will you have this completed?

Now bring it all together using the SMART goals
table:

<table>
<tr><td>Final goal:

</td></tr>
</table>

Chapter
5
Prioritize & Schedule

Don't let that one thing that you are not enjoying suck up all of your time, especially if it is a job that you hate going to. Take some time away from it to work on other projects, this way you are slowly but surely building your freedom and reshaping your happiness. Creating and sticking to a regular schedule will help cultivate positive habits and keep you on course towards experiencing the natural growth you declared for your life's dreams and goals.

Work out a strategy for what you will be doing with your time. A schedule does not only produce positive habits, it creates balance between our work and our life. If you find that the strategy isn't working, change it up and try something new. For instance, if you are allocating time in your schedule to work on a side hustle and you notice that the time you have scheduled is not enough, give yourself some more time, even if it means taking time away from something else. This is the essence of scheduling and prioritizing, something will have to give. Each of us is given the same amount of time in a day—24 hours. What we choose to do with it will determine the outcome of our life.

To avoid burnout, it is important to take breaks. The last thing you want is to overwork yourself and go right back to that place of unhappiness because of too much stress. The idea with Magnetic Mondays is to build momentum for the week ahead; you want to keep the cart in motion.

Developing time management skills is a journey that needs practice. Here are some strategies for using your time:

Dedicated Workspaces

Determine a place where you can maximize your concentration and be free of the distractions that family, friends or hobbies can bring. If you tend to look at your phone every few minutes, keep it away from your workspace until you are ready to make calls or send messages. Also, find a backup space that motivates you, like a library, a garden or even a coffee shop where you can work quietly. A change in venue may also bring extra enthusiasm and inspiration.

Create an Activity Log

Start by keeping a log of your work and the time you spend for a few days to get a sense for how efficiently you are working. Your log will also help you recognize whether you're doing your most important work during the right time of day. You may have more energy and concentration at night rather than in the morning; therefore, you may need to schedule your work accordingly.

Logs are also useful for helping you identify non-core activities that distract you from meeting your goals and objectives. For example, you might spend far more time than you think surfing the internet or chatting on the phone with friends without never really realizing it. When you see how much time you're wasting on such activities, you can change the way you work.

Create a To-Do List

Creating and prioritizing your to-do list will keep you on track week after week. Make sure you add the most important tasks on your list first and account for everything, including family, personal life and business. To-do lists are essential if you're going to beat work overload, be better organized and experience less stress.

Two Ps for Inspiration

Finding inspiration is the gateway to our inner creativity. It can lead to the most amazing outcomes, not only for ourselves but for others. Inspiration can come from anywhere and it isn't always found in the most obvious places. It can come from places of desperation, disappointment or satisfaction.

So, find what inspires you by:

1. Going to see **places** – get out there and experience some of the natural wonders the world has to offer. It's really amazing how big and beautiful the world is. You can do this with little to no budget. If all you can afford are free venues within your city, then start there. Don't limit yourself to only one place or one travel destination. There is no single place that can inspire you and you don't need to travel halfway across the world to find your inspiration.

2. Meeting **people** – I find that I am more inspired by people than I am by places. Depending on your personality, your source of inspiration could vary;

maybe you are more inspired by places than you are by people. Nonetheless, try to have conversations and get to know people. Where did they come from, what's their story and how do they spend their down time? I started doing this with my neighbors; surprisingly, I learnt that they were able to retire ten years early. They travelled to many places and are currently enjoying a comfortable life doing exactly what they want. If that's not inspiring, I don't know what is.

Perhaps you will find something within you that you never knew existed. Maybe you will find the inspiration to start a cause, open a business, write a book or volunteer. All you need is that one inspirational moment to light the fire.

End of chapter exercise:

Take a look at your life and start penciling chunks of time, depending on what is important to you. Start to plan time for building your career and redesigning the life you want. Perhaps you need to dedicate time to writing a resume, creating a social media presence, starting a business or joining an interest group.

I suggest approximately 5-10 hours per week. If it's not possible, go at your own pace.

Time				
Monday				
Tuesday				
Wednesday				
Thursday				
Friday				
Saturday				
Sunday				

Chapter
6
Build Your Network

Before you can progress in life, you must take a moment to consider your relationships. What type of people are you around? Are they progressing? How do they make you feel? Do they understand you intimately? Do they support your dreams and aspirations?

Most importantly, what is their general outlook in life? Being surrounded by people who are always negative and who always make excuses for why their life is so miserable is no good for you. This type of environment is only holding you back. Of course, there are situations that are beyond one's control, but that is not what I am referring to. I am referring to the people who find an excuse for why they are constantly late to work or people who complain that they were overlooked for a promotion but never actually took any initiative to lead or bring about change. Those are the people you want to steer clear of because they have either lost their passion or have yet to find it. These types of friendships and relationships are toxic because they infect your mind, your thoughts and actions.

We use our bodies to communicate. The gestures, facial expressions, and body postures we make are social signals, ways of communicating with one another. For example, when you see someone smiling, your mirror neurons for smiling fire up, too, initiating a cascade of neural activities that evoke the feelings you typically associate with a smile. You don't need to make any inference from what you are feeling, you experience immediately and effortlessly (in a milder form) what the other person is experiencing. Mirror neurons respond to the actions we observe in other people. For this reason, you need to surround yourself with people who are strong, positive and inspirational. Surround yourself with people who will cheer for you even when you aren't winning.

In clearing the clutter of toxic relationships, you begin by simply spending less time with these people. Rather than engaging in a conversation that is demeaning, you simply let these people know that you are working on a brand-new transformational project, knowing that the project involves working on yourself. It does not mean that these people are bad; it just means that they are not good for where you are heading in your life right now.

Before you start networking and building new relationships, you have to work on changing your thoughts. If you feel like the world is always against you, you will bring this thought with you. Perhaps you feel like you have been overlooked because of what you look like or because of where you have come from but try your best not to focus on this. Press on knowing who you are and the good work you are able to produce. Shake off all the rejections, shake off all the statements that left you feeling worthless and inexperienced. Focus instead on who you are and what you are able to do. Although there are over seven billion people in the world there is no one out there who is like you. Take a moment to consider this. Consider what you do and the way in which you do it. This is your starting ground for standing out. Ensure that the quality of your work shines through in the way you treat others. People will always remember the way you make them feel and in relationship building this is key.

Get out there!

The most important step in building your network is networking. That means you actually have to get out there and become involved.

Here are some tips for finding your next networking opportunity:

- Research the company or person you want to work with.
- Look for events they are hosting or causes they support. Try to go to these so that you can meet people from that company. Face-to-face is always best.
- Look at what activities/events other members of the company attend and arrange to be there. Forming relationships with employees within the company can be a good source for referrals.

If you can't find people to network with, it may be an opportunity for you to host a meet-up or a conference and/or collaborate with others. Think about how many other people may be in need of the same type of networking collaborative community that you are seeking.

Bring the right supplies

Whether you are meeting with one or many people, you always want to put your best self forward and you always want to be comfortable.

- Dress appropriately. (Try to find out if there is a dress code. If you are unsure the best approach is business casual.)

Dressing well is what attracts people to you initially, not your intellect, personality or sense of humor. Think about that for a minute. Before you ever get the chance to say a word, you attire will be your first impression and could potentially be a nonverbal icebreaker. This is a great way for you to take some of the pressure off of your initial introduction, boost self-confidence and improve your overall ego. Trust me, during a time of continuous failure or when you're fighting to survive, a little boosted ego just might get you through the next stretch. But don't be intimidated by the need to dress well. Dressing well does not mean that you've got to dress up in expensive suits or outfits but wear what is clean, well put together, fits, flatters and most importantly is appropriate for the audience.

- Wear comfortable shoes. Avoid heavy bags and uncomfortable shoes. Most conferences and networking events will require some walking around and extensive standing. The last thing you want is to be distracted by an aching shin.
- Bring an iPad, notepad or pen. You may learn new information or come up with new questions to ask the people you meet, so you want to write down these questions at the time they cross your mind.
- Have printed copies of your resume and/or contact card.
- Have a camera (take selfies, check in and share on social media). Even if you don't want to share on social media, you should take a few pictures of yourself at the event. You never know when you might want to refer to these or post at a later time.

When trying to stand out in crowd, especially at a networking event, always focus on being yourself. You want to initiate a conversation with people at the event, come prepared with questions so that you have something to talk about. Always remember you need to constantly remind people who you are and what you do without being pushy or obnoxious. Try to get the contact information of the people you are meeting with so that you can send them an email or give them a call. Begin the conversation by introducing yourself and then talking about the value you bring to your work. End the conversation with saying, "I'd really like to learn more about your company and the kind of impact it is making on its customers. Perhaps we can set up some time to talk." If the person you are networking with wants to know more about you or how they could work with you, they will give you their contact information or the contact information of someone else you can connect with at their company.

Treat every meeting as a networking opportunity. Whether you are on the bus, the train or standing in a line at the coffee shop, treat the people around you with kindness and respect. You never know who they are and what mountains they are capable of moving for you. These days it's very difficult to determine who is a good person to network with, especially if you have never had the chance to meet them before.

Listening is an essential ingredient in building a string of long-term networks. The idea with networking is to build meaningful connections and relationships that go way beyond the first meeting. So, make an impact. You do this by giving your undivided attention to the person you are meeting. Stand at a comfortable distance from that person so that you can maintain eye contact during the conversation and try to genuinely smile. If you are bored by the conversation, it's a good chance for you to guide it in the direction you want by asking direct questions.

People suddenly disappear or go dead silent after a phone or email conversation, especially after a discussion about a job or partnership opportunity. This behaviour can become very annoying so do not let it get to you. Send a follow-up email or call a maximum of two times. If you have received no response, I would assume that the employer or potential work partner is not interested. Therefore, you should move on.

Never take anything for granted. Celebrate your wins and recognize people who are genuinely engaged and interested in you and what you have to say. These types of encounters are few and far between.

Social platforms are another tool you can use to build relationships. Connect with people who are in a professional group that resonates with you. Even if you are not too good with tech, having a social profile is the only way to say you exist and you have a voice. These platforms are great for showcasing your expertise and your interests. You can do this by simply posting educational "How to" videos or creating a blog post about things of your personal interest. If you don't have a lot of time to spend on social networks, check in on a weekly basis by simply "Liking" or "Commenting" on someone else's post. If you want to progress and you want to be known, you have to constantly remind people of who you are. Social media posts allow you to do this from practically anywhere in the world with a data connection.

In addition, creating an online presence on social media provides a great medium for you to keep current with all that is happening globally. It's a great way to learn new strategies and methodologies without ever having to leave your home. These days information is free but service comes at a premium price, so take advantage of all the free information that is at your disposal. Consume it and grow with it.

Chapter
7
Happiness

Gallup has been measuring international employee satisfaction for almost two decades. In total it has polled 25 million employees in 189 different countries. The latest poll gathered information from 230,000 full-time and part-time workers in 142 countries. According to a Galllup poll, 85% percent of workers worldwide admit to hating their jobs and 62% of workers are described as "not engaged", meaning they are "unhappy". We are checked out, sleepwalking through our days, putting little energy into our work.

If you struggle with being happy in the workplace, here are some quick methods to turn that frown upside down!

1. Develop a positive outlook – Savor the little moments, enjoy relationships and conversations with colleagues, be accepting of feedback.

2. Avoid toxic and negative people – Being in a workplace with people who are always complaining about the salary or culture of your organization is like standing in the room with an irked skunk. Without even noticing it, you, too, start becoming stuck with negativity.

3. Be optimistic – Change your thoughts from *'Everything sucks, I can't do anything to change this. It's all my fault.'* Developing an optimistic outlook means thinking about yourself and your world in unlimited, flexible terms.

4. Celebrate & embrace your wins – Remind yourself of who you are and your personal wins. *"I am the best at this! I've got this, I graduated with a double major, I made the Dean's list. I accelerated my career and got that that leadership position within a year of working at this company."* These

daily affirmations will allow you to cultivate an attitude of gratitude even when things are not going well.

5. Perform random acts of kindness – "The best way to find yourself is to lose yourself in the service of others." - Mahatma Gandhi. CEO and social media marketer Kim Garst has her own version of the "never work for free" debate. Garst argues that if you don't value your time, nobody will and so you should charge for your talents. But a little bit of charity can go a long way, as can volunteer work with those less fortunate than you—regardless of how much money you yourself have.

Volunteer to be part of programs at work. For example, if your company participates in a charitable event, take time to be part of that. Whether it is a run for cancer research or volunteering in the program for *Take our kids to work'*, do it as an act of kindness; do it because you want to be part of a change. Don't do it because your VP will be there and it's a good opportunity for him to notice you.

Avalee Prehogan, Senior Regional Manager at Robert Half, says that, "happy workers are more loyal, more productive and make tangible contributions to their organizations." In fact, there have been a number of studies done over the years to prove this notion. According to a recent workplace happiness study by Robert Half, the top three drivers of happiness for Canadian workers are:

- Having pride in one's organization

- Feeling appreciated for the work they do

- Being treated with fairness and respect

Most importantly, don't give up on your ideas—believe in yourself and know that you deserve it. If you have had an idea for something you should build, develop or improve then work on it. It will bring you great pleasure to labour for your passion.

Take a deep breath … and stand tall.

Tony Robbins describes it as Power Posing where the individual stands tall with his chin up, shoulders back and hands on the hips.

In fact, a recent study by Harvard School of Business showed that preparatory power posing can serve as a simple, free, nonverbal tool that has the potential to be adopted by and beneficial to almost anyone, including those who are chronically powerless due to lack of physical resources or hierarchical status.

What's the science behind Power Posing and how does it help boost your happiness level?

In primates, expansive, open postures reflect high power, whereas contractive, closed postures reflect low power. Let's think about what the posture of a person who is happy and confident might look like. Well, they might stand tall, their head would be up, and they might even wear a smile on their face. Adopting high power poses increases explicit and implicit feelings of power and dominance, risk-taking behavior, action orientation, pain tolerance, and testosterone (the dominance hormone) while reducing stress, anxiety, and cortisol (the stress hormone).

Not only do strong authoritative postures reflect power, they also produce it.

Created by Gan Khoon Lay from Noun Project

So, the next time you need to prepare for an interview or presentation, take two minutes to pose like Superman or Superwoman. Chin up with eyes looking ahead, arms on the hips and taking long deep breaths, focus on a moment that you are proud of.

Money can't buy happiness

For many of us, money may seem like the answer to all our problems. Unfortunately, we all know that very old adage "money can't buy happiness". This is especially true in our careers. According to Maslow's Hierarchy of Needs, an individual is motivated to fulfill five basic needs, physiological, safety, social, esteem and self-actualization. According to Maslow, once the need for survival is fulfilled you move to the next level of motivation. Under this theory money would be recognized within the safety category (or a base need for behavior). In other words, we are motivated to work when we receive compensation. When we have money, we feel secure because we have a resource we need to survive. When the physiological needs are met, we then move on to the next levels of the hierarchy until we get to the point of realizing our full potential. This is especially true in the workplace, think about an employee who earns enough to furnish the lifestyle he wants but lacks the respect and recognition he desires from his colleagues or superiors.

Such an environment would not motivate an employee; neither would it make him happy. The fact is many people face these issues in the workplace each day. So, don't let money be your primary motivator in life. Instead, try to use money as a medium to enjoy the life you want. Live a life of clarity and purpose.

Use money to create your financial freedom

There is a general misconception that financial planners are for people with money, but I think people with little to no money are the ones who need them most. These days you can get financial advice from a bona fide advisor for little to no cost. Most banks usually offer this service to its customers for free, the most you would need to do is schedule an appointment.

Since finances touch every aspect of your life, you want to work with a financial planner who will look at your unique financial goals and tailor a plan that is just for you. In your conversation you should consider addressing topics such as budgeting, debt management, tax and retirement planning. Do not be afraid to say it if you feel that you don't have enough to meet your goals. It is the financial planner's job to come up with a strategy that will work for you.

However, before you meet with a financial planner there are some things you can start doing to save for a rainy day. Full disclosure; there are really only two ways to have more money—**make more** or **spend less**.

Since it's easier to spend less than make more, here are four ways that you can start saving:

1. For each paycheck you receive, set up an automatic deposit into your savings account. You can decide how much your budget allows.
2. Ensure all your bills are paid on time to avoid late penalties including bad credit.
3. To avoid impulsive buying, give yourself some time to think about it. A wait period of 24 hours will give you time to consider if the product is really necessary.
4. Avoid using debit or credit cards and put yourself on a cash budget. Use cash to pay for smaller expenses such as coffee, meals or even shopping at the mall. The psychological effect of watching money leave your hand may deter you from spending as much as you would if you were using a card.

Happiness is an emotion just like sadness or anger, so we shouldn't try to chase it as though it is some untouchable shadow. Instead, embrace happiness as a state of mind by looking for moments of contentment.

Chapter
8
Individual Development

Don't ever feel bad for wanting or needing to improve. If you want to overflow with abundance, then you need to find ways to fill yourself up.

Sean McPheat, Founder and Managing Director of MTD Training, advises that you should, "Sharpen your skills and be ready. Identify gaps and areas for self-development, be prepared and willing to try out new things". It's okay to switch career paths and decide to do something different, we are not one dimensional and neither are our aspirations.

You need to be clear on what your strengths are and what complementary strengths you need from others. This means taking an inventory of your current skills and areas for improvement or growth. Think about what courses you can take to enhance your chances of a promotion or to get to the position you want. It is not always some technical or specialist course that is required. Sometimes it's working on your soft skills. Soft skills relate to how you work with others (whereas hard skills relate to you, in isolation, as an individual). For example, your soft skills would be your strong work ethic, the way you communicate with others and the way you problem solve while your hard skills would be your professional certifications, your degree or diploma or your proficiency in multiple languages.

In a recent interview Avalee Prehogan, Senior Regional Manager at Robert Half, said, "Sometimes it's more about finding a work environment and culture that you really enjoy going to every day. We spend so much of our lives at work, so it's important that our workplace is one where we often feel fulfilled. A good fit isn't just about having the right experience and background for a role. It goes beyond qualifications to include temperament and soft skills." Employers value soft skills because they enable people to function and thrive in teams and in organizations as a whole. Perhaps you need to work on your presentation skills so that you can communicate better to an audience. Being self-aware by knowing your shortcomings is great way to identify areas for professional development training.

If you find something you want to work on, there is an abundance of development resources, easily accessible for free, through the World Wide Web or even through government agencies. These days, you can train from home for most certification programs or you can join a virtual classroom if you need the extra support. There are several videos on software training out there and many meet-up groups are popping up just about everywhere. There is literally no end to the amount of information circulating out there; for this reason, you should reach within to find those untapped potentials that haven't been honed yet.

Learn from your failures

No one likes to fail. In fact, many people will avoid taking on new challenges or risks because of fear of failure. For this reason, many workers stay in the same job for years without ever stepping up or out to learn more. But it is very unlikely you will experience growth unless you are willing to take a leap. Think of Thomas Edison, as an inventor he made numerous unsuccessful attempts at inventing a carbon-based, high-resistance filament for the light bulb. When a reporter asked, "How did it feel to fail 1000 times?" Edison replied, "I didn't fail 1000 times. I've just found 1000 ways that won't work." The light bulb was improved with 1000 steps. Could you imagine if we were this relentless with our goals? Could you imagine if we learnt from each mistake and tried a different way after each failure?

I remember, when I was first starting out in my career, I had no idea how to use Microsoft Outlook. I was the receptionist at a well-known company when one day the CEO called and asked me to send him an invite to a meeting that was planned by another executive. My initial thought was, *"This is simple enough, I'll just add him to the invite and press send."* However, when I added him and hit 'send', I was prompted to 'send updates only to added or deleted attendees' or 'send updates to all attendees'. Not understanding the message, I decided to remove all the other employees and send to the CEO only. By doing this a cancellation notice was sent to all and only the CEO was on the invite. Well, as you can imagine, an abundance of emails and phone calls came in asking if the meeting was cancelled and of course the CEO was wondering why he was the only one in the meeting. The story ends with me being at the company for only a day, followed by some lessons in Microsoft Outlook. Nowadays I have my phone handy to either do a quick Google search or call a friend when I am not certain what to do. The moral of this story—don't be embarrassed by your failures because we all experience them whether young or old. Having many years of experience does not make us free of mistakes. Learn from them and move on.

Lean on others

Oftentimes we are self-reliant or we are too proud to ask for help. But sometimes we need to lean on the expertise and knowledge of others to get to our next level. For many of us this can be a humbling experience, especially when pride starts to get in the way. But life has a funny way of teaching us these lessons of community and friendship. We weren't created to figure it out all on our own and, quite frankly, no one individual has all the answers. People are generally willing to help, especially if it is getting someone connected to the right job opportunities. If you have been asking people and there hasn't been any positive response, don't lose hope. This just means one of two things, you aren't qualified for what you are asking or you aren't asking the right people. Either of these situations can be changed. You may need to down grade to a lower level job before you can get to the one you want or you may need to speak with some different people who have the authority to influence hiring decisions.

If you think it is too difficult to get in touch with the right people, take a look back in history at the people who paved a path for many to follow. Airbnb was inspired in 2007 by two roommates living in San Francisco who couldn't afford to pay the rent. To make some cash the pair decided to turn their loft into an area that could fit three air mattresses. Along with the mattress and a night's sleep was the promise of a breakfast. Fast forward to today, the company is worth somewhere around 30 billion dollars. This would not have been possible if they did not see the need to lean on each other and influence others for partnerships and investments.

Psychologists contend that all humans have an inborn need for other people. As a result, we need to have people who we can ask for help, people who we can vent to and people who will listen to us. Maybe one person can meet all these needs or maybe you have different people for different needs. Perhaps the person who is always willing to listen may not be able to help your situation, but they are able to offer you comfort by just listening.

Sometimes, we just need an outlet, a friend, a brother or a sister that will listen to us protest about life, our boss, our career or our failures. Things are not going to always go smoothly, especially when you are trying to make a huge shift in your life. So try not to hold it all in; complain, have a pity party if you must, and then get back on the horse.

Chapter
9
Perseverance & Patience

Many of us have the desire to accomplish great things, but how many of us have the patience to wait for the fruits of our harvest?

Perseverance and patience are two difficult things to put into practice and can only be done in one way— that is to keep doing.

Created by Stephen Borengasser
from Noun Project

Everybody wants FAST—fast food, fast forward, fast access— but steady and slow wins the race. When it comes to big wins and things that really matter in life, we must exercise patience. Be persistent about your goals and patient enough to wait for them to manifest. That desire for a stress-free, high-income career should never be given up on.

Recently, I stumbled upon the story of Tyler Perry who was inspired to write. He grew up in an impoverished household. He had no connections, no network and he certainly wasn't fed with a silver spoon. He saved every penny to stage his first play for what he hoped would be a packed audience. However, for six years many of the seats remained empty. The people in the audience were people he knew; they were friends and family that came to support him. There was hardly anyone new in the audience. Can you imagine how he felt, that feeling of rejection, fear and second-guessing his decision to put all of his savings into something that was not succeeding? There must have been something that kept him going. He persevered and had patience for his work because of his passion for storytelling. He believed enough in his dreams to be tenacious about them. After sowing many seeds, advertising, reaching out, building relationships and persisting, that same play would sell out at a local run forcing the production to move to the much-admired Fox Theatre. It wasn't until lately that I got to know about him, now that he is an acclaimed playwright, screenwriter and actor. That is the thing with success; nobody sees the toil and months or years of struggle.

Most business owners and successful career professionals will tell you that they made a five-year plan for what they wanted to achieve, which means that they gave themselves time to learn as much as they could. They were not consumed by the instant gratification monkey (that desire to have things right away). They aimed to be happy and positive each day without allowing that five-year plan to consume every other area of their lives. This should be your objective, too; don't become so obsessed by the goal that you lose sight of its purpose. Allow yourself to live out that purpose every time you are given the opportunity.

If your purpose for attracting your ideal career is so that you can travel more, don't spend five months locked in a basement working only on that strategy. Doing this would be counterproductive. Instead, make plans to travel to a new city or town within your country. Get some nice deck furniture and sit in the backyard or on the balcony. Take time for yourself and take time to get away, even if it's a staycation or stroll in the park. Create opportunities to enjoy the little things because running on the treadmill of life can become exhausting if you don't take some time out to catch your breath.

Finally, don't get lost in the comparison trap. Remember a tree bears fruit in its own season. Celebrate others' success, even if you feel like you have been given the worst of situations.

What song are you singing while you wait?

It is my firm belief that everybody needs two songs in their back pocket, a **fight song** and a **feel-good** song. A fight song keeps the fire within you burning long after the feeling you first started out with dwindles. It stimulates something within that makes you want to tear down those metaphorical walls. On the other hand, a feel-good song lifts your spirit and brings you to a place of tranquility and contentment.

The psychological effects of music are mind-blowing. It has the capacity to energize and increase endurance. Focusing on our favourite song combats demotivating brain signals associated with fatigue or boredom. Upbeat music has been shown to increase positive feelings. Essentially, much of music's power lies in its ability to elicit emotional reactions and enhance mood.

According to Tony Robbins, music is one of the greatest gifts we have to change our mental and emotional state. Use it strategically to produce different types of state.

You can listen to music while you create your website, while you work on your resume or while you update your social media profile during your job search. Whether we recognize it or not, music has nonverbal, creative, structural, and emotional qualities. These are used in a therapeutic relationship to facilitate contact, interaction, self-awareness, learning, self-expression, communication, and personal development.

Perseverance takes a lot of willpower and consistency, so having a song to sing when you feel like the climb is daunting will keep you going.

Chapter
10
Momentum

This brings me to another very important topic when we talk about attracting our ideal career. Simply defined, momentum is mass in motion. So, you cannot have momentum unless you decide to start moving and keep moving.

If you think of your life as a chaotic roller coaster with ups and downs, there is a lot that you can model, and I would like to present a positive spin on that. The first hill being the highest point of the roller coaster is very important. This is where all the energy for the ride originates. Likewise, you will experience some stress and frustration on your climb to success. You might even get scared and wonder why the climb is so slow. But all you really need to do is focus on getting to the top of the hill, even if you're only able to give one hour per week to your dream, even if you've been rejected, even if it's painful. Your passion and perseverance will be enough to carry you to the top of the hill.

However, once you get to the top of the hill, everything will start to come together. Be sure to take a moment to take in the view. According to the law of conservation of energy, energy can be neither created nor destroyed (lost); energy is only transferred from one form to another. So, when the cars are at the peak of the hill, they have the highest potential energy. As they race down the other side of the hill, the potential energy becomes kinetic energy, and gravity takes effect, speeding the cars along the track. Likewise, as you gain traction and start to feel success you will find energy there, enough to carry you through the entire ride.

Most successful people worked on an idea for many years before it was finally realized. What may appear to be overnight success is actually many hours, days, weeks and months in the making. Once you're at the top and have put in all the hard work, it will start to appear like all things are falling into place; it may even start happening so fast that you may not be able to comprehend it all.

So, you keep the momentum going through hard work. Know that momentum takes time to build. It may not always be easy, it may even feel like you are carrying an unbearable weight, but keep going on towards your passion. Surround yourself with people who will not only cheer for you but will also alleviate some of the burden by carrying the weight with you. I have a friend who would stay up with me all night so that I could finish a proposal for the next day. That same friend would take the time out of their day to run my meetings or address questions from my clients.

Slow down if you must, but never stop. It's just like Newton's First Law of Motion: The tendency of a body in motion is to keep moving; the tendency of a body at rest is to sit still. In other words, it takes a lot less work to keep moving once you have some momentum than it does to start moving from a stand still. I noticed this was particularly true when I started knitting a scarf, I worked on it for a few days and then I left it off to do something else. When I came back a few weeks later to finish up the scarf, it felt like I was learning to knit all over again, I didn't have the same energy as I did when I originally started working on it. It was gruesome, I felt discouraged and demotivated, and to be honest I never finished that scarf. I understand that attracting your ideal career and knitting aren't the same thing, but hopefully you understand the principle in this.

Seth Godin writes, "Many of us fear too much momentum. We look at a project launch or a job or another new commitment as something that might get out of control. It's one thing to be a folk singer playing to a hundred people a night in a coffeehouse, but what if the momentum builds and you become a star? A rock star? With an entourage and appearances and higher than high expectations for your next work?... Deep down, this potential for an overwhelming response alerts the lizard brain and we hold back."

It may seem like you have waited for so long and BOOM it's all happening. But what has happened is you have transferred all that energy from climbing the hill, you've changed your mindset, defined your purpose, set goals, practised patience, persevered, grown and learnt along the way.

Now you are ready to attract the career of your dreams!

End notes

I hope you are inspired to put into action at least one thing you've read in the book as,

"I truly believe that professional success and happiness are directly linked to our ability to act."

~ Mariana Pachai-Bose

About the Author

Mariana is passionate about empowering people who want to transition into a fulfilling, purpose-driven career which satisfies their professional aspirations. As an immigrant, she struggled for many years with trying to fit in and finding her ideal career. She had dreams, like all of us, and wanted to create a lifestyle where she could work, spend time with the family, and still have the freedom and money to travel. But the truth is, once she started out in her career, all those dreams quickly died. She had no idea how to grow professionally, regain balance or manage stress.

Then what might seem like the flip of a switch was the exact thing she did to transform her life. She knew it was either sink or swim, so she changed her outlook, became positive, and took action. She challenged herself to extend beyond what she knew by doing research, networking, and asking a lot of questions.

Fast forward to today, she is an accomplished author, HR consultant, and founder of Pave Your Path Career Transformation Coaching. She has helped clients regain balance and attract their ideal career by looking within.

Now, her life's mission is to help people take charge of their life, regain confidence, and create their own happiness.

To Contact the Author

75

Email: mariana@pypcoaching.com

Website: www.pypcoaching.com

Telephone # 647-503-5541